AF410623

As co-founder of Nomi Network, an anti-trafficking workforce leader, I'm in awe of Kimia Penton's *Power, on Purpose*. Its genius grants permission to claim your voice and empower others, turning positional power into collective force for change, while insights on inner circles, culture, and radical authenticity build intentional lives that protect peace and amplify global equity.
– Diana Mao Kelly
President and Co-Founder, the Nomi Network

Kimia leads with authenticity and intention. In every space she enters — academic, professional, or creative, she elevates others by helping them see their own potential more clearly. *Power, on Purpose* is both a mirror of who she is and a guide for anyone ready to lead with meaning and impact.
– Dr. David Parks
University of Texas, Dallas

In a world that rewards conformity, this book makes a compelling case for Authenticity as the most radical form of leadership. Kimia Penton is one of the most authentic individuals I have ever met. Her kindness, courage, and humanity are not just values she speaks about — they are how she leads. Through personal storytelling and powerful insight, this book shows how returning to yourself becomes a powerful roadmap for better leadership, greater alignment, and a more humane way of holding power.
– Dustin Jones
Chief Human Resources Officer

Power, on Purpose names the cost of performing success and reminds us that leadership begins the moment we choose alignment over approval.
– Rebeca Riofrio
Chairwoman, Parliamentary Society for Arts UK, COO SIGULP, CEO Art in Fusion TV

Kimia Penton represents authenticity and purposeful leadership in its truest form. This book is simply Kimia being herself — opening up, sharing her journey, and offering principles that guide how she lives, leads, and serves the world.
– Taopheek Babayeju
CEO, iCentra, Founder of The TAB Foundation and LeadPreneur

Kimia Penton is the embodiment of power with intention. I've witnessed her claim a rare kind of leadership—one born of creativity, courage, and the willingness to be fully seen after doing the deep work required. In *Power, on Purpose*, she doesn't posture or perform; she opens the door and shows you how she became. This book is an invitation into creative leadership that is grounded, conscious, and alive—where influence is not accidental but authored with heart. Kimia is the kind of leader this moment in history has been waiting for.
– Elizabeth De Moraes
Global Presence and Branding Strategist and Speaker/Media Personality

Kimia has written a book that reflects how she lives – authentically integrated, whatever room she's in. And at the same time, she's given you an excellent primer on leadership.
– Andy Harrison
Fortune 10 HR leader

Power, on Purpose is sacred courage. When authenticity leads and purpose guides, power becomes light, creating space for others to rise into who they were meant to be.
– Mylinh Luong
Servant Leader

Power, on Purpose is more than a book — it's an invitation to stop shrinking, stop performing, and stop outsourcing your identity to roles or expectations. Through honest storytelling and practical frameworks, it guides you back to the kind of power that comes from clarity, alignment, and being fully yourself.
– Arman Amiri
Sr. Partner and Business Development Lead

Power, on Purpose

Where Authenticity Becomes Radical Leadership

Kimia Penton

Published by

Kimia Q Productions LLC

Kimia Q Productions LLC

Power, on Purpose
Where Authenticity Becomes Radical Leadership

This edition (softcover) ISBN 979-8-9944252-0-6

This book is intended for informational and inspirational purposes only. The views expressed are those of the author and are not intended to replace professional, legal, medical, or psychological advice.

Cover photography by Kauwuane Burton

Edited by Anahita Penton and Andrew Luke Penton

Printed in the United States of America

Contact information: contact@kimiapenton.com

To my children, Anahita and Luke,

may you always know your worth, trust your inner
voice, and choose a life guided by purpose, courage,
and love

How to use Power, on Purpose

I wrote this book to share my development journey and as encouragement and an invitation for you to deepen your internal awareness and strengthen your self-mastery. My hope is that these pages spark honest reflection, meaningful insight, and the courage to choose alignment over expectation as you shape a life that is authentic, fulfilling and impactful.

When I refer to power, I'm referring to the conscious, grounded ability to choose, influence, and act in ways that align with your values for fulfillment and positive impact. Using your power, on purpose, is the intentional use of your voice, influence, and energy in ways that are values-driven, and rooted in self-awareness rather than fear or performance.

Each chapter and the ending of the book have pages for notes as well as a glossary of key terms, because this book is meant to be lived with. Use it as a journal. Pause when something resonates, jot down what comes up, and give yourself permission to explore it further. I'm cheering you on as you grow, stretch, and step more fully into who you are becoming. Wishing you much success, fulfillment, confidence, and purpose in your life and work. When you've completed the material, if you have a story, insight, or moment you'd like to share, I'd love to hear from you. Reach out to me and my team at: contact@kimiapenton.com

You've got this! Kimia

Contents

The Moment I Disappeared

Chapter 1 – The Moment I Disappeared

I remember the exact moment I realized I had been performing my own life. It wasn't during a major crisis or some dramatic turning point. It happened quietly, in a conference room on the eighth floor of a corporate tower. The kind of place where success has a scent: fresh coffee, perfume, and power. The meeting was running smoothly, my team respected me, and my name carried some weight. On paper, everything was perfect. I had done everything I was supposed to do. And that was the problem.

As the conversation carried on around me, with its polite corporate nods, data slides, and subtle performance of confidence, I felt my body go still. Something inside me whispered, *where did you go?*

I had done everything right. First-born daughter in a traditional Middle Eastern family. The one who sets the example, carries the expectations, keeps the peace, and makes the sacrifices look effortless.

I grew up understanding that worth was measured in achievement, obedience, and how gracefully you could juggle both. So, I did. I graduated with honors, married young, built a beautiful family, and earned the promotions. Kept the smile. Checked every box my parents and relatives had prayed over. And yet, somewhere between becoming who everyone needed me to be and who I actually was, I vanished.

The irony was that I had achieved power, or at least the version of it I was taught to pursue — titles, recognition, and stability. But I didn't feel powerful. I felt like a well-trained actress in a role that had run too long. Every time I silenced my truth to keep the peace, chose approval over self-respect, and ignored my inner voice, I chipped away at my own presence and expression.

That day in the conference room, something in me refused to stay silent. Not loudly, not yet, but enough for me to hear it. A voice, quiet but certain, said: *You've mastered this role, but you abandoned yourself.*

That realization hurt more than any failure ever could. Because it meant I had been betraying the one person I was born to be in exchange for a version of myself that made everyone else feel comfortable.

It's a familiar story, especially for those of us who are raised between different cultures. We're taught to honor family, culture, and reputation — and I do. But we're rarely taught how to honor ourselves within them. To be the first-born daughter is to inherit an invisible crown of responsibility, one that gleams with pride but weighs heavy with guilt. You're expected to make your parents proud, to make the family look good, to be strong, kind, wise, educated, and selfless all at once. And if you do it well enough, you're rewarded with love, validation, and constant, quiet exhaustion.

For years, I had mistaken obedience for peace, performance for purpose, and exhaustion for devotion. Until one day, I saw the difference between being a *good girl* and a *free woman.* That moment became the beginning of *Power, on Purpose.*

This isn't a book about rebellion. It's about **returning**. Returning to truth. To alignment, the state of living and leading from your true values and identity instead of expectations of others. To the kind of power that doesn't depend on permission.

It's about leading your life the way it was meant to be led: not as a performance, but as a living, breathing expression of who you are. Because one of the greatest acts of leadership we can perform is the decision to stop abandoning ourselves.

The Art of Unlearning

Chapter 2 – The Art of Unlearning

After many years of collecting my accomplishments like armor, I realized that true power doesn't come from adding more — it comes from *unlearning*.

From leading a global team within a Fortune 10 organization to stepping onto the TEDx stage, teaching at the university level, speaking on global platforms, and accepting my first board position, each milestone carried external credibility and visible success. Yet achievement alone does not equal fulfillment. In several of these moments, I realized that I was still operating from my learned behaviors, meeting expectations, and fulfilling roles rather than fully inhabiting my power and leading from a place of deliberate identity and purpose.

Unlearning for me wasn't a single moment of revelation. It was a slow, sacred unraveling and peeling back of layers I didn't even know I had built.

At first, I did what I had always done: I studied. I enrolled in courses, attended workshops, and I listened to motivational talks. I devoured books on mindset, growth, leadership, and psychology. I became my own research project, determined to understand the patterns that had shaped me.

But this time, I wasn't learning to perform better. I was learning to *be* better for myself.

Through the guidance of mentors and coaches, I began to see the blind spots that had kept me on autopilot. I took self-assessments that revealed my strengths, values, and my energy drivers. Some results affirmed what I already knew; that purpose and connection mattered deeply to me. Others were uncomfortable truths, showing how often I minimized my voice to maintain harmony.

So, I started tracking my days. Not just what I had accomplished, but how I felt. I began writing down what drained me, the meetings that left me depleted, the people-pleasing habits that stole my energy, the self-doubt that whispered I wasn't doing enough. And alongside that, I noted what made me come alive, the moments I felt fully present, joyful, creative, and in flow.

Music and mentoring students. Speaking from the heart. Building something meaningful with people I love. Helping others see their own power.

Patterns began to emerge. The things that drained me were always tied to *performance*. The things that fueled me were tied to *purpose*. It sounds simple, but profound: my energy was a compass. And when I stopped ignoring it, it started pointing me home.

That awareness changed everything for me. I stopped chasing titles and started chasing alignment. I gave myself permission to redefine my success: not as perfection or applause, but as peace.

For the first time, I asked: What if power wasn't about control? What if it was about *clarity*? And what if purpose wasn't something to find, but something to *remember*? What if it was something that had been quietly waiting beneath all the expectations I had carried?

As I continued my journey of unlearning, I did so with a deep kindness toward myself and the people who shaped me. With time, I realized most of us were doing the best we could with what we knew, operating from our own survival patterns, inherited beliefs, and blind spots. Understanding that softened me. It allowed me to release blame and instead choose growth. And as I stepped into greater authenticity, changing how I spoke, how I worked, how I loved, and how I stood up for myself, those shifts became an invitation. The people around me began to see what was possible. My development inspired them to take a closer look at their own hopes, their own patterns, and their own untapped courage. This collective growth motivated me to continue unlearning.

Unlearning the rules that kept me small, the belief that productivity equals worth, and the idea that love, and approval must be earned. Unlearning the habit of putting everyone else's priorities above my own.

Unlearning the fear that boundaries were selfish and instead learning to embrace them as one of the most sacred expressions of love for myself, and love for relationships I want with truth, not resentment. Quelling the instinct to stay silent about difficult topics, to shrink myself to keep the peace, and instead to encourage authenticity and growth.

One mindset that kept me small early in my career was the belief that I was simply lucky to have a job and that an ideal role wasn't truly available to me. With experience and as I began to recognize the value of my contributions, that belief slowly lost its grip. I became more discerning about the roles I pursued and more intentional about where I chose to invest my energy.

Instead of chasing titles or opportunities out of fear, I focused on developing and mastering my craft and partnering closely with leaders who supported my growth. Before applying for a role, I took time to reflect on whether I respected the organization, believed in the team culture, and felt comfortable with the leadership. In interviews, I wasn't just trying to be chosen; I was listening for fit. I wanted a role where I could make meaningful contributions and feel genuinely fulfilled.

That shift from feeling grateful just to be included in my personal or professional life, to choosing with intention, changed the trajectory of my career and relationships. It helped me to learn that fulfillment isn't something you stumble into by accident; it's something you build *on purpose.*

This has been the slow, courageous reclaiming of who I really am beneath the roles, the conditioning, and the expectations and the decision, repeatedly, to choose alignment over adaptation. This conscious decision to love, work, and lead in a way that is true to who I am, stopped my reshaping to fit external expectations or environments.

A Japanese concept that resonated deeply with me and supported my journey of redefining myself is *Ikigai,* which loosely translates as "reason for being". The book *Ikigai,* written by Héctor García and Francesc Miralles is a helpful guide for how to implement this concept in your life. Rather than asking who we are meant to become, this framework gently invites us to begin with what is already within us: what we are naturally good at, what we can be paid for, and what the world genuinely needs. Starting here removes pressure and replaces it with curiosity and clarity. As part of the unlearning process, *Ikigai* is a practical and insightful tool, helping untangle identity from expectations, roles, and outdated narratives. It reminds us that purpose is not to be chased or performed, but something we uncover as we work to realign our strengths, contribution, and values.

The journey of unlearning is never comfortable. But it is sacred work. Because when you begin to strip away the noise of what the world told you to be, you finally hear the music of who you are.

Notes & Reflections

Notes & Reflections

3

Home and Close Relationships

Chapter 3 – Home and Close Relationships

Where Authenticity is Practiced and Strengthened

Home is the place where our truest self tries to speak first. Long before our titles, responsibilities, or expectations enter the picture, home is where we learn what love feels like, what safety means, and what belonging requires. It is also where we learned the earliest versions of performance—the gentle ways we bend ourselves to keep the peace, to meet expectations, and to avoid disappointing the people we love.

Reading back through the story of my life, I can see how much of my identity was formed in those early rooms: the tone of voices, the unspoken rules, the roles we quietly adopted without ever realizing they were shaping us.

We all needed the same things growing up: love, safety, consistency, belonging, a place in the tribe, the feeling that we mattered. And because those needs are so primal, we shape ourselves around whatever gives us the best chance at receiving them. Some of us become the achiever. Some become the peacemaker. Some the caretaker. Some the invisible one. I never consciously chose my roles; they were woven into me in the quiet spaces between family gatherings, the whispered expectations, the reward systems at school, and cultural norms.

And like so many of us raised between worlds, with a different culture from our parents, I learned early that harmony came from staying agreeable and self-monitoring rather than self-expression. What we practice at home becomes the blueprint for how we show up everywhere else.

The First Patterns

Family is our first classroom. It teaches us how love is given, how conflict is handled, what mistakes mean, and how worth is assigned. It teaches us whether our voice matters or whether it's safer to stay silent. If the conference room in Chapter 1 was where I realized I had disappeared, then home was where that disappearing act began. Not because anyone intended harm, but because our very first ecosystems (our families), teach us how to survive, how to love, how to protect ourselves, and how to earn approval.

When I first learned about Shirzad Chamine's Positive Intelligence® Framework years later, it all suddenly made sense. The Saboteurs (mental habits that may undermine our well-being while trying to protect us) we carry into adulthood were first formed in those earliest spaces as survival patterns, and we can overcome them with Sage powers like empathy and curiosity. Sage powers are described as our highest mental and emotional capacities that lead to better decisions. The framework helped me to realize that my Hyper-Achiever didn't come only from ambition; it also came from believing my worth was tied to my performance. My Pleaser didn't come only from kindness; it came from fearing that love could be lost if I ever disappointed someone. Understanding this didn't make me blame my family; it made me understand them more deeply. They, too, were living out patterns handed down to them.

Everyone in a family system (parents, siblings, and caregivers) has been shaped by their conditioning, fears, dreams, and belief systems. Understanding this helps us see the complexity of human nature. It helps us recognize patterns without internalizing them as destiny. You can honor your roots without letting them dictate the direction of your growth. If you're on the journey of understanding yourself and your family norms, I highly recommend the Positive Intelligence® Framework as a powerful tool for self-awareness and communication.

Authenticity in Adulthood

Authenticity in our adulthood begins when we stop living through the lens of old roles and choose who we want to be today. The choice to consciously define ourselves instead of repeating past patterns is an act of personal power.

Our true self is most visible at home because home is the place where we drop the mask. And it is often the place where our unhealed patterns appear first. If you really want to know someone, look at how they treat the people closest to them. Look at how they resolve conflict. Look at who they become when they are stressed, tired, vulnerable, or unfiltered.

Practicing authenticity at home is sacred work. You can't fake emotional maturity with the people who know you best. They see the parts you haven't healed yet.

They see the patterns you are still unlearning. And they see the glimpses of who you are becoming.

I'm very passionate and intentional about nurturing my closest relationships, and I have never been satisfied with sweeping things under the rug or with saying, "this is just how we are". Power at home, for me, is soft and strong. It's not pushy. It's discerning, loving, and focused on having positive influence and lasting impact. It's kind, not nice. Kindness requires honesty, courage and some difficult conversations. Perhaps the most important place to honor this is in your home.

My adult children, Ana and Luke, are two of my closest friends. When they were young, I resisted the urge to act like their friend. As a parent, I had rules that were in their best interest, and I would communicate them clearly while explaining that I loved them too much to be a lazy parent. My rules, behavior, words, and actions were consistent and intentional. Practicing alignment at home requires intention. It means allowing your values, not your moods or old patterns, to guide your actions.

Practicing alignment might look like:
- Speaking calmly even when you're triggered
- Choosing curiosity instead of defensiveness
- Repairing conflict instead of avoiding it
- Saying "I need a moment" instead of exploding
- Creating space for vulnerability
- Listening without rehearsing your rebuttal
- Respecting your own limits and others'

- Letting your children see you apologize, reflect, and grow
- Being honest without being harsh
- Holding space for others without losing your boundaries

At home, projections of power often show up in how we speak during tense moments. Broad, sweeping statements like, "you always do that" or "you never help with this" can quickly feel accusatory and create distance. I've found that approaching those moments with curiosity instead of certainty helps build bridges and invites shared understanding. For example, "you never help with picking up the dishes", can be positioned as, "can we talk about how we share the responsibility of cleaning up? I'm feeling stretched and could use your help."

These small, daily choices can change the entire emotional climate of the home. What's important is the willingness to show up with intentionality, authenticity, and consistency, and to show up even when it feels inconvenient or uncomfortable.

Breaking Cycles with Compassion

Growing into your power sometimes means that you disappoint the people who benefited from your silence, compliance, or your self-sacrifice. As you become more authentic at home, you may:

- Say no more often
- Express needs you once suppressed
- Redefine family roles

- Establish new boundaries
- Stop rescuing or over-functioning
- Refuse emotional manipulation
- Disengage from old conditioning
- Ask for reciprocity and respect

This can create tension at first, but tension is not failure. Tension is growth. My son Luke tells me that there's a reason they're called "growing pains". Out of these growing pains, we can create space for greater awareness, deeper connections, and the breaking of cycles that no longer serve us.

A powerful way to break cycles is with compassion. Compassion doesn't excuse harmful behavior; it expands understanding. It helps you see that in many cases people were doing the best they could with the awareness, tools, and emotional maturity they had at the time. Your evolution can inspire others, even if it challenges them initially. When you grow with love, you create an environment where healing becomes contagious.

When Home Becomes a Sanctuary

As I've continued doing my own inner work, I've noticed something beautiful happening: our home feels lighter. We're quicker to resolve conflicts. Conversations are easier. There is more laughter and honesty, and more room for each of us to be who we are without tiptoeing around old wounds. When my family and I watched Brené Brown's *Atlas of the Heart* together, something shifted for all of us. Naming emotions gave us a shared language. It softened misunderstandings. It helped us see one another not through judgment, but through compassion and with clarity. We all also found the conversations around anger as a mask, or secondary emotion to protect hurt, fear, shame, grief, and powerlessness to be very eye opening.

Emotional literacy changed the way that we all communicated, as if someone finally turned the lights on in rooms we had been navigating in the dark. I refer to *Atlas of the Heart* as I navigate close relationships and encourage growth and meaningful connection. It's another powerful companion tool I recommend. It's important to build a home on authenticity, psychological safety, and compassion because these homes become:

- A sanctuary
- A grounding place
- A source of strength
- A reflection of your integrity rather than survival

And when your home is grounded, everything else expands—clarity, creativity, courage, the capacity to show up in the world with purpose. This is where personal power stabilizes. Power begins inward, but it takes shape at home. And from that rooted place, your power flows into the world with clarity, integrity, and purpose.

Notes & Reflections

Notes & Reflections

Power and Social Presence

Chapter 4 – Power and Social Presence

Your Voice in the Spaces you Move Through

Power is not only who you are within yourself; it is also who you become in the spaces you enter. Social presence is the quality of your energy, the weight of your voice, the clarity of your boundaries, and the way you influence the room without abandoning your authenticity. It is your ability to hold your sovereignty while navigating personalities and egos, alongside expectations and dynamics with grace, firmness and intention.

Every space that you move through; your home, workplace, community, friendships, or stages you speak on, reflects to you the state of your inner alignment.

For years, my presence in a room was shaped by the conditioning I carried: the constant expectation to be agreeable and to keep the peace. I believed that belonging was something earned through silence, compliance, or predictability. But the truth is, real belonging is impossible when you abandon yourself to obtain it. It is created when you can stand fully in who you are and allow others to meet you there without losing yourself to their approval or their reactions. Social presence becomes powerful when you understand that your voice is not a disruption; it is a contribution. And real power can never flow through a voice that's afraid to speak.

This chapter is about reclaiming your voice as a compass. It is about stepping into service, not self-sacrifice; connection, not conformity; authenticity, not performance.

Belonging, Service, and the Courage to be Truly Seen

Belonging is one of the deepest human needs, and sometimes one of the most misunderstood. We often confuse belonging with fitting in. Fitting in is performative. Belonging is presence. Fitting in requires altering ourselves. Belonging requires revealing ourselves.

When you enter a space rooted in authenticity, your presence becomes a service. People feel grounded around you. Your energy isn't demanding attention; it's creating permission. This is the essence of meaningful community: the exchange of authenticity that widens connection and amplifies impact. A great example of a life led by these principles is one of my favorite musicians and creatives, Jon Batiste. Jon embodies what it means to lead from authenticity. When he enters a space, you feel it: grounded, open, joyful, human, and creating permission for others to be fully themselves. Through his music, joy, and unapologetic truth, he turns authenticity into service, reminding us that meaningful community is born from the exchange of realness. If you ever have a chance to see him perform live, I highly recommend it. The musicality, joy, message, energy, and intentionality are truly inspiring.

Service and Presence

Service is not overextending, over-delivering, or over-functioning to meet everyone's expectations. Service is using your presence, your gifts, your clarity, and your compassion in ways that contribute to the spaces you inhabit, serving from overflow and not from depletion.

When you begin moving through the world with authenticity, focus, and purpose, something beautiful happens—the right opportunities, the right people, and the right spaces of impact naturally rise to meet you because your inner state becomes a beacon. You don't have to force your way into rooms that aren't meant for you; instead, you find yourself guided toward places where your gifts can genuinely be of service.

A few years ago, I joined a local nonprofit in Dallas serving people who are often overlooked. As I showed up and volunteered in the areas that lit me up, I met some incredible people who shared the same values and a few of them have become some of my closest friends. One of them really *saw* me, not just what I was doing but why I cared so deeply. She excitedly told me, "You have to meet my friend," who happened to be the founder and CEO of another nonprofit. She introduced us, we instantly connected, and now I'm on that organization's advisory board. She knew exactly who to connect me with because she saw my heart, my passion, and my purpose. When you're living with authenticity, the right people recognize you without you having to explain a thing.

I also had the chance to join the board of directors for a professional organization in Dallas. As I browsed through the open positions—VP of Finance, VP of Marketing, VP of Programs—none of them felt like home. But when I saw *VP of Outreach*, something in me lit up. Community, connection, and service are the threads that run through everything I do, and that role fit perfectly with who I am. I raised my hand, trusted that pull, and spent two deeply meaningful years serving in that position. Thankfully, the other roles were filled by people who had a passion for those functions. It was another reminder that when you choose what resonates with your purpose, the experience becomes enriching in ways you never could have planned.

Stepping into roles that truly fit me taught me how different it feels to show up from a place of wholeness instead of serving out of a sense of obligation. But even with the best intentions, there are habits in social or professional settings that quietly drain our power without us noticing. In this next section, we'll explore four of these pitfalls to avoid.

Protecting your Power from People-pleasing

People-pleasing is one of the most subtle and socially rewarded forms of self-abandonment. It trains us to negotiate our needs, to believe that harmony is more important than honesty, and that peace is worth the cost of our power.

But protecting your power doesn't mean becoming indifferent, unkind, or unavailable. It means choosing truth over approval. It means recognizing when your energy is leaking into places it doesn't belong. It means understanding the difference between being supportive and being self-erasing.

To protect your power, reclaim your boundaries not as walls, but as clarity. Boundaries are not barriers to connection; they are the conditions that make healthy connection possible. They are acts of love—for yourself, for your relationships, and for the version of you who refuses to live in resentment or exhaustion. A powerful skill you can develop is the ability to say *no* with grace. A clear, kind no honors both your boundaries and your relationships. It lets you protect your time, your energy, and your purpose without creating conflict or guilt. A simple phrase like, "Thank you so much for thinking of me but I have other commitments at the moment," is enough. You don't owe a long explanation or a justification. Your no can be warm, respectful, and confident. And every time you practice it, you reinforce the message that your time and energy matter. This way, you start building relationships where your power is respected, not extracted.

Say Less, Speak When it Matters

A powerful shift in social presence is learning the difference between speaking to be understood and speaking to be impactful. Not every situation requires your voice. Not every conflict needs a reaction.

Saying less is not about withholding or shrinking. It is about becoming intentional:
- Pausing instead of reacting
- Observing before responding
- Speaking at the right time
- Being clear and concise

When you speak from grounded clarity, your words carry weight. You communicate as a leader, not a pleaser. You say what is necessary and then you stop speaking. Silence becomes a tool, not a threat. Space becomes a strategy, not a void. People learn to pay attention when you speak because they can feel the intention behind your words.

Emotional Power and Managing Emotions

Have you ever been in a meeting where someone completely lost their cool and control, disrupted the meeting and distracted from the agenda? It's awkward and not a great display of emotional intelligence. Emotional intelligence is about stewarding your emotions. It's about knowing the difference between:

- A reaction rooted in fear or a response from truth
- A silence rooted in avoidance or a pause rooted in discernment

Your emotional world holds immense power, but only when you hold it with awareness. When you master your internal landscape, you will become harder to trigger, easier to trust, and more grounded in your interactions.

Emotional regulation doesn't mean that you become emotionless. It means becoming self-aware and grounded. It means understanding that your tone, your timing, and your delivery are just as important as your message. It means choosing expression that expands connection rather than erodes it.

For example, instead of reacting in an emotionally charged meeting the day before, something as simple as saying, *"Is this a good time to catch up on yesterday's meeting? I noticed it was intense, and I may have some ideas that could help,"* sets the tone for clarity, support, and collaboration. It signals care without tiptoeing, and leadership without force. Communication, at its core, is emotional leadership. You are leading yourself first and then guiding the conversation.

Navigating Personalities and Egos

Every space contains a mosaic of personalities: assertive, shy, loud, withdrawn, rude, enthusiastic, analytical, competitive, sensitive, avoidant, visionary, insecure. Social presence requires the ability to meet these personalities with curiosity, not defensiveness.

You cannot control other people's egos, reactions, or emotional patterns. But you can anchor your own. Anchoring means:

- Not absorbing other people's urgency
- Not matching other people's chaos
- Not shrinking in the presence of dominance
- Not inflating in the presence of insecurity
- Not taking on someone else's emotional state

This is the heart of relational power: you maintain your center even when someone else has lost theirs. Your presence becomes power—guiding connection, shaping community, and raising the standard of every space you enter.

Notes & Reflections

Notes & Reflections

Power Through Your Circle

Chapter 5 – Power Through Your Circle

Authentic Connection as a Source for Strength

There's a point in every healing journey when you look around and realize something undeniable: the people closest to you help shape the way you see yourself. They shape what you believe is possible, and they shape how brave you're willing to be. For a long time, I didn't understand how deeply my inner circle influenced my power. I thought I had to do everything alone. Carry my dreams, navigate my doubts, and climb whatever mountain was in front of me with quiet determination. I believed independence was strength. But independence without support is survival, not power.

The truth is, your purpose might begin within you, but it expands through the people who recognize it. Your inner circle becomes the soil your growth rises from. And if the soil is dry, rocky, or depleted, even the strongest seed will struggle. But with the right people who are rooted in honesty, love, and alignment—you grow faster, stronger, and with far more clarity than you ever could alone.

For most of my life, I gravitated toward relationships that were familiar rather than aligned. Familiar felt safe. Familiar felt expected. But familiar also kept me small. I didn't realize I was surrounding myself with people who loved the version of me that was performative and held the peace, but not necessarily the version of me that wanted to expand. I was surrounded by people who would only reach out to me when they needed something, and historically, I had felt obligated to help. As I began unlearning the patterns that shaped me, my relationships began to shift. Some friendships grew deeper than I imagined; others fell away quietly, almost gracefully, as if making space for what was coming next.

That's the thing about becoming more authentic: the people who can meet you there rise to the surface, and the people who can't naturally drift. It's not personal—it's energetic truth.

Your Inner Circle

Your inner circle isn't defined by history or proximity. It's defined by resonance. These are the people who see you without the performance, who hear the sound beneath the words, who celebrate your growth even when it takes you in a new direction. They don't need you to shrink for them to feel comfortable. They don't confuse your boundaries with rejection. They don't mistake your ambition for arrogance. They want you whole, not convenient. They care more about your well-being than how easy, agreeable or useful to them you are.

Those rare, steady souls don't fix or rescue you— they reflect you back to yourself, reminding you who you are when life tries to make you forget.

But building a powerful inner circle takes something foundational: self-respect. Without it, you'll keep choosing people who fit your fears instead of your future. You'll keep tolerating disrespect in the name of keeping the peace. You'll keep giving more than you receive because you're afraid that having needs makes you burdensome.

Self-respect is the quiet voice inside that says, *"My peace matters. My needs matter. My worth is not negotiable."* When you honor that voice, you'll see that your relationships shift. You stop apologizing for your boundaries. You stop explaining your value. You stop betraying yourself in the name of connection.

Finding and Nourishing your Friend Circle

My friend group is one of the areas of my life I'm most proud of, and I don't take it lightly. I'm often asked how to find friends as an adult, because it *is* harder than when we were younger, when proximity did most of the work for us and shared classrooms, activities, and schedules made connection effortless. As adults, friendship requires intention. It asks us to offer friendship before we expect it, to make the first move when we notice something we admire or a value we share, and to lean into curiosity instead of hesitation. This can look as simple as inviting a coworker to lunch, asking a neighbor over for dinner, or showing up to a community or volunteer event where shared purpose creates natural connection. Too often we wait to be chosen, when what builds community is choosing first. Don't be afraid to get to know someone. A question, a genuine compliment, or an invitation can become the beginning of something meaningful. Connection doesn't arrive fully formed. It's built, one brave reach at a time.

Kindness not Niceness

A transformative lesson I learned as I navigated my relationships was the difference between being nice and being kind. Niceness is rooted in performance—it avoids discomfort, hides truth, and keeps the peace at your expense. Kindness is rooted in honesty. It's compassionate and clear. Kindness allows you to say no guilt-free and yes without resentment.

The more I practiced authentic kindness with myself and others, the more I found fulfilling relationships. I started attracting people who valued truth over comfort, accountability over avoidance, depth over performance. The conversations changed, the energy changed, and I changed.

And then something remarkable happened: I began to see my relationships as teachers. Every single one. The ones that strengthened me taught me joy, trust, and reciprocity. The ones that hurt me taught me boundaries, discernment, and emotional maturity. The ones that fell away taught me how to let go with grace.

Relationships reveal the places we're healing and the places we're hiding. They show us what we've outgrown and what we're ready to grow into. They stretch us, soften us, and make us more human. Have you ever noticed yourself holding back your thoughts in one relationship while feeling more grounded and freer in another? If so, it may be worth taking a closer look at why that is. Are you worried about being judged or starting an argument in one, yet feel safe to be fully open in the other? These contrasts are often gentle signals, guiding us toward the relationships and the version of ourselves that invite honesty, growth, and wholeness.

But even with the healthiest people, conflict and hurt are possible. Emotional maturity isn't about avoiding those moments. It's about learning to see them clearly. *Let people be who they are.* Not who you want them to be. Not who their potential whispers they could become. Who they *are* right now.

Mel Robbins' *Let Them Theory* beautifully captures this: let people be exactly who they choose to be. Let them show you their patterns, their limits, their capacity, their effort—or lack of it. Let them cancel, not show up or misunderstand you. Let them reveal their values through their actions, not their promises. When you stop trying to manage, fix, or reinterpret someone's behavior, you free yourself to see the truth with clarity instead of hope. *Let them*—not because you don't care, but because who they are today is the only information you can trust. It's all information, and information is power.

Healthy Endings –a Path Forward

When a relationship can't offer the resolution or repair you need, you can still choose a powerful path forward.

Healthy endings are a powerful form of self-respect. It's the practice of giving yourself the closure that someone else may never be able to offer because they simply don't have the emotional maturity, capacity, or courage to meet you there. A healthy ending doesn't require confrontation, explanation, or an agreement. It's an inner decision: *I choose peace over confusion. I choose clarity over chaos. I choose myself over the hope that they will suddenly become someone different.* When you bring yourself resolution, you free your heart from waiting for someone else's growth. You stop rehearsing conversations that will never happen. You reclaim your power by closing the chapter with compassion, honesty, and grace—on your own terms. This applies to personal and professional relationships.

The right people feel like wind at your back, not gravity on your shoulders. They don't dim your voice, they amplify it. They don't drain your energy, they protect it. They don't compete with your growth; they rise with it. These are the people who expand your courage, elevate your standards, and remind you of your power on the days your confidence feels thin.

Our Internal Red Flags

Our external connections reflect our inner state and journey towards self-mastery. Self-mastery is the process of knowing yourself deeply and regulating your inner world with intention. It's a journey that requires the courage to address blind spots to our own internal red flags. It's uncomfortable to look at our own patterns. This is where a healthy inner circle can support us by pointing out behaviors and patterns we may need to address. When we find ourselves repeating the same situations, dynamics, or disappointments, it's worth pausing and asking what we might be contributing to the cycle. If our story repeats with different people or circumstances, we are the common denominator. Owning that truth isn't about shame, blame or self-criticism; it's about reclaiming agency. Examples of internal red flags include repeatedly feeling drained or anxious around certain people, ignoring your gut feeling or intuition, regularly saying yes when you mean no, tolerating inconsistency or disrespect, and deflecting feedback instead of reflecting on it.

The moment we acknowledge our role and power; we can move forward in a healthier and more productive direction. This is where self-mastery becomes essential. The only person we can truly control is ourselves—our behaviors, boundaries, expectations, and timing. Self-mastery is a work in progress that allows us to step into a life led by intention, clarity, and personal power rather than repetition and frustration.

This theme of self-mastery and accountability is also woven into my music. My song *Red Flags* begins with finger-pointing and calling out the warning signs we see in others. But ultimately, it turns the mirror inward, acknowledging that growth requires us to address our own behaviors while maintaining healthy boundaries. It's a reminder that empowerment isn't just about what we tolerate from others, but about the necessary standards, awareness, responsibility and the power we bring to every relationship. If you enjoy music with a message, I invite you to listen to my *Unfiltered* album, a collection of original music on all streaming services that encourages reflection and the journey back to self.

Your Circle as a Determinant of Destiny

Your inner circle is one of the greatest determinants of your destiny and directly influences the quality of your life. As you continue your growth and development, choose your people with intention, clarity, and with self-respect. And trust that the right ones will recognize you the moment you show up as your whole self. These are the people who cheer you on, lift your spirits in times of stress, and help you to see yourself the way you truly are. When you choose people who honor your truth, your power becomes unstoppable.

Notes & Reflections

Power and Value

Power and Value

Money, Worth, and Influence

I still remember standing in our kitchen as a child, desperately wanting to fit in with my classmates. At school, My Little Pony was everything. My friends arrived each day with brightly colored ponies, and together we filled the playground with elaborate stories and imagined adventures. I wanted to belong to that world, but our reality at home looked different. My parents were rebuilding our lives after losing everything in an unexpected international move, and during that season, new things were rare. The focus was on essentials, not extras, and new toys were not a priority.

Still, I gathered my courage and asked. I remember saying, almost apologetically, "Mum, Dad, can I have a My Little Pony? Everyone else in my class has one." They asked me what it was, listened carefully, and told me they would think about it and do their best. I left the room, but I didn't go far. From the hallway, I overheard them talking quietly about how they might pay for it, whether it was necessary, and how they could make it work if it truly mattered to me. Hearing that conversation changed something in me. In the middle of a difficult chapter for our family, their care and thoughtfulness filled me with a deep sense of gratitude and pride. Knowing I was heard mattered more than the toy itself, and by the time they finished talking, I had already decided I wouldn't bring it up again. It no longer felt important.

The next afternoon, after school, I saw my dad approaching with a brown paper bag in his hand. It was crumpled and unmistakably shaped like a small horse. I knew immediately what it was. He handed it to me with a wide smile, and I tore the bag open to find a simple plastic pony, gray with white hair. No bright colors, no famous branding, no logos. None of that mattered. It was my dad's choice, and I loved it completely.

That moment stayed with me and decades later, that pony still sits on my nightstand. I've moved across countries and cities more times than I can count, but I've never lost it. When I showed it to my dad recently, we smiled at the memory we still shared. Long before I had language for it, I learned something that day about money, meaning, and well-being. I learned not to anchor my sense of worth or security in material things, and I learned that intention, care, and stability matter far more than appearances. That lesson became the quiet foundation for my life, and I didn't lose my contentment, whatever my circumstances in the seasons that followed.

Managing Money with Intention

Years later, as I began my professional career, I believed money was neutral. It was practical and necessary, but impersonal. I told myself it had nothing to do with purpose, power, or identity, that it lived in a separate box far removed from meaning and fulfillment. Over time, I realized how incomplete that belief was. Money, when unmanaged, has a way of quietly shrinking your world, while money handled with intention expands it in profound ways.

I'm not encouraging the chasing of wealth for the sake of wealth or tying your worth to a bank balance. This is about reclaiming agency and building a foundation strong enough to support the life you are trying to grow. Purpose needs stability to breathe, and without it, even the most capable and driven people can find themselves operating from pressure instead of choice.

When your finances are constantly stretched, life feels heavier. Creativity tightens, courage wavers, and options narrow. You may still be talented and ambitious, but your decisions are shaped by urgency rather than alignment. Financial clarity changes that dynamic. There is a quiet confidence that comes from knowing your bills are paid, your needs are met, and you have margin. Margin to rest, to say no without panic, to walk away from situations that no longer fit, and to invest in yourself, your ideas, and your growth.

As I stepped into my professional life, my relationship with money began to shift. I became less focused on what I could acquire and more curious about how I could manage what I had with intention. I wanted to be a good steward of my resources, to avoid the pitfalls of a lack or scarcity mindset and understand how money could support my life rather than control it. Not as a symbol of success, but as a tool for stability, freedom, alignment, and possibility.

Money for Future Stability and Generosity

I'm not a financial expert, and I've never approached money from a place of perfection. What I've learned has come through experience, observation, and small, consistent choices over time. The practices that grounded me financially, and ultimately allowed me to use money in ways that strengthened my sense of power and purpose, were simple but meaningful: avoiding debt wherever possible, choosing to live beneath my means so I could create margin, committing to save a percentage of my income each month, and setting aside a percentage to give toward causes I believe in each month. These habits weren't about restriction; they were about creating breathing room and building trust with myself. There were seasons I said no to trips, upgrades, and comforts so I could say yes later to financial freedom.

An impactful benefit of financial stability is the freedom to be generous without experiencing fear, stress, or resentment. When your foundation is solid, you can support causes you care about, help others without sacrificing your own well-being, and use money as a tool for positive influence rather than a constant source of anxiety. That's power through the effective use of money. Money itself is not power, but the freedom and influence it creates often is.

There is so much I wish I had understood earlier, but one of the most important lessons has been that it is never too late to begin. Saving or donating a specific percentage may not feel realistic at every stage of life, especially in the beginning, and that's okay. What matters is starting where you are. Even small, consistent steps toward saving can create future stability, and generosity grows naturally as capacity increases. Over time, these habits compound, not just financially, but emotionally, reinforcing a sense of agency, confidence, and calm that supports every other area of life.

Delayed Gratification and Longterm Freedom

The books *Your Money or Your Life* by Vicki Robin and Joe Domínguez and *The Richest Man in Babylon* by George S. Clason had a deep impact on how I came to understand money and its relationship to freedom. Both offered simple but powerful reframes that stayed with me, particularly the idea of delayed gratification and the practice of paying yourself first. Delayed gratification is one of the least glamorous and most transformative skills you can develop. It is the practice of choosing long-term freedom over short-term relief, of resisting the urge to soothe discomfort with spending, and of learning to sit with the pause instead of filling it with debt. These books also challenged me to see money not as something to consume impulsively, but as stored life energy, a resource that represents time, effort, and choice. By prioritizing savings before spending and resisting the urge for immediate reward, I began to experience a quieter form of financial freedom, one rooted in intention rather than accumulation. These teachings reinforced that true wealth isn't about excess, but about alignment, the ability to make decisions without fear, and the confidence that comes from knowing your money is working in service of the life you want to build.

Another book that inspired my perspective on money is *The Stoic Path to Wealth* by Darius Foroux. Darius reframes money as a byproduct of clarity, discipline, and character rather than something to be chased or used as a measure of worth. He emphasizes the importance of focusing on what you can control—your choices, habits, and mindset, while adopting a long-term perspective rooted in patience and consistency. Through a Stoic lens, wealth becomes the natural outcome of thoughtful decision-making, offering a grounded and sustainable approach to financial well-being.

Financial Management as Self-Respect

Managing your finances well is an act of self-respect, a way of saying that you matter enough to create stability for yourself and that fulfillment is not only emotional or spiritual, but practical and grounded.

When you are financially grounded, you are less likely to disappear. You become harder to shake, less inclined to abandon yourself out of fear, and more capable of standing tall, not because you have more, but because you are no longer bracing for collapse. This is the power of enough: enough clarity, enough discipline, and enough foresight to build a life that can hold your purpose, not just imagine it. Money, when aligned, does not own you; it supports you, allowing your influence to expand naturally, steadily, and in ways that endure.

Notes & Reflections

Notes & Reflections

Power in Organizations

Chapter 7 – Power in Organizations

Authenticity as Radical Leadership

I am fascinated by organizational psychology—not just the theories or research, but the lived reality of how people show up at work. We spend so much of our lives inside organizations that, in many ways, they become mirrors: reflecting our confidence, our insecurities, our sense of belonging, and the stories we tell ourselves about our worth. For better or worse, work shapes us. It influences how we see ourselves, how we measure our impact, and how safe we feel to bring our full humanity into the room. And the more I've grown in my career, the more I've realized that the most powerful thing you can bring into any organization isn't your résumé, awards, your credentials, connections or your performance; it's your authenticity.

Authenticity becomes radical leadership in today's organizations because being your true self in systems built on conformity is an act of courage. Most people lead from expectation; doing what they believe they "should" do, following unwritten rules, and trying to avoid judgment. But radical leaders lead from truth. Their decisions come from clarity, their values, and their purpose. Not from pressure or fear. Leading from expectation creates compliance. Leading from truth creates courage.

For authenticity to become radical leadership, you must begin with yourself. You've got to know what you stand for, where your boundaries are, what energizes you, and what drains you. You've got to understand what matters to you, not because it looks good on paper, but because it lines up with your inner compass. As you grow, your influence naturally grows. And when you live with purpose and boldness, your authenticity stops being a personal preference and becomes a leadership strategy. I've sat in rooms where I could feel the pressure to soften my opinion, to make my message more palatable. Each time I chose clarity instead of approval, my voice shook a little less the next time.

This is what makes authenticity radical. It's radical not because it is extreme, but because it goes to the root. Radical comes from the Latin *radix*, meaning root. Radical leadership asks you to build the outer world from your inner world first. It's integrity over image and purpose over pressure.

Leading From the Inside Out

Radical leadership begins within you. Leading from the inside out means that in every room or situation, you're cultivating:

- Emotional awareness (responding, not reacting)
- Purpose clarity (knowing your *why*)
- Nervous system regulation (staying grounded, present, and steady)
- Inner narrative control (choosing your self-talk)

My journey has been challenging at times with multiple international moves, balancing artistry with corporate leadership, and resisting the temptation to shape shift in each new room, environment or industry. By practicing authenticity with adaptability, I've learned to hold my voice in rooms that weren't built for me, and I hope for that to be a model of empowered presence on my terms.

The Myth of the Neutral Leader

So many leaders try to mask themselves at work. They wear a professional persona, dilute their identity, or cultivate perfection to avoid criticism. They hide their humanity behind credentials. But these masks come at a cost. They create burnout, inconsistency, distrust, and limited influence. People can feel when you're performative, or faking it, even if they can't name it.

Authenticity, on the other hand, builds connection. It deepens trust because people experience you as real, consistent, and grounded. When you lead from who you truly are, you create emotional safety and the foundation of collaboration, innovation, and loyalty. People follow leaders they trust.

A closer look at Authenticity

Authenticity is not about telling everyone everything or wearing your emotions without discernment. Emotional intelligence is needed to know what's yours to share, when to share, and in ways that serve the moment. This requires intentionality and not impulsivity, especially in the workplace. For example, instead of venting frustration in the middle of a team meeting, you might acknowledge feeling concerned, pause to gather clarity, and choose to address the issue constructively in a follow-up conversation where solutions, not emotions lead the discussion.

Authenticity is not about being abrasive or demanding under the guise of keeping things real. Authentic communication means expressing truth with respect, self-awareness, and consideration for the impact your words have on others. In the workplace, this might look like giving direct performance feedback with clarity and care rather than delivering blunt criticism that puts someone on the defensive and shuts down growth.

Authenticity is not about refusing to adapt to new environments or ways or working. Statements like, "this is just the way I am" can block your growth and development. For example, a leader may prefer independent work but still choose to engage in collaborative tools and team processes because growth sometimes means stretching your habits.

Authentic leadership is about congruence—being the same person in every room. It's when your inner truth matches your outer expression. Your words, actions, values, and boundaries create a coherent leadership presence. I noticed this most when I stopped saying yes to projects that looked impressive but left me drained. My calendar got quieter, but my presence got stronger.

Authentic leaders demonstrate integrity not just through what they say, but through the energy they bring into a space. They embody their values even when no one is watching. They show consistency in who they are, not just in what they produce. This creates grounded influence, the kind that doesn't need a title to be felt.

Many organizations reward conformity, professional masks, and survival patterns. People are praised for endurance, not authenticity, empathy or connection. They are rewarded for productivity instead of purpose. So, when someone shows up truthfully, with clarity, compassion, boundaries, courage, leadership, and authenticity, it disrupts the norm.

Being real in systems that expect performance is a radical act. It means:

- Speaking truth with kindness, even when it's uncomfortable
- Holding boundaries without apology
- Choosing values over popularity
- Creating psychological safety
- Encouraging humanity over performance
- Looking beyond appearances or surface level

In this environment, authenticity isn't a buzzword. It's a form of leadership that liberates others to be real too.

Accountability

We also need to be real and take accountability in the face of challenges in the workplace. Accountability requires a courageous willingness to look honestly at our own impact, especially when the feedback is uncomfortable but valid. In moments like these, ego can be a tempting armor, but humility is the truer strength. Maintaining accountability means staying open, listening without defensiveness or anger, and acknowledging where our actions or inaction may have fallen short. It requires understanding that perception matters, not as a threat to our identity, but as valuable data that helps us grow into more effective, trusted leaders.

Throughout my career, changing roles has often meant stepping into moments of rebuilding—forming new teams, supporting organizations through turnaround, and redesigning processes that no longer serve the work. What's hardest is when progress doesn't come as quickly as I'd like, especially when the real work involves technology shifts, team changes, or cultural change. Those transformations take time, and in the middle of them, the distance between effort and visible results can feel discouraging and personal. This is where accountability and humility can become an anchor: remembering what you signed up for, staying grounded in the long view, and committing to both short-term progress and long-term impact with healthy communication with your teams. When we release the need for immediate validation and stay focused on purposeful change, we lead with clarity, resilience, and intention and set a powerful example even when the work tests us.

The Benefits of Radical Leadership

Radical Leaders can be a powerful force for organizational change by transforming organizations from the inside out. They:

- Build teams grounded in trust rather than fear

- Attract talent that aligns with mission and values
- Navigate conflict with clarity instead of reactivity
- Create spaces where innovation and creativity thrive
- Lead with long-term purpose, not short-term performance

These leaders are culture shapers. Vision expanders. Their presence becomes an anchor that supports the entire system.

As a radical leader:

1- Trust Becomes your Competitive Advantage. Authenticity builds emotional safety, the foundation of collaboration. Teams move faster, think more creatively, and become more loyal when they trust the person leading them.

2- You Lead with Clarity and Energy Instead of Exhaustion. When you're not shapeshifting, you free up enormous mental and emotional bandwidth. You become energetically consistent, and consistency is magnetic.

3- You Attract Aligned Opportunities and People. Radical authenticity filters out what drains you and draws in what nourishes you. You find meaningful work, values-aligned teams, supportive communities, and purpose-driven roles. Your power becomes focused and directional instead of scattered.

4- You Create a Legacy of Personal and Collective Freedom. You're liberated from people-pleasing, fear-based management and systems that diminish human potential.

Two leaders that come to mind as I write this chapter are Bobby Herrera and James Rhee.

Bobby Herrera, author of *The Gift of Struggle*, embodies values-based leadership grounded in authenticity and courage. Years ago, I came across his book at an airport and read it on the flight home. I found it to be extremely impactful. When I invited him to meet with my team, he generously said yes and led a powerful session on authentic leadership. His message that integrity and struggle shape meaningful leadership, left a lasting impression on how we show up for our work and one another.

James Rhee, author of *Red Helicopter*, offers a powerful example of human-centered leadership in practice. By intentionally pairing kindness with rigorous business metrics, he led the turnaround of Ashley Stewart when the organization was on the brink of bankruptcy. As Chairman and CEO, his approach reshaped the financial performance as well as the culture. He demonstrated that empathy and accountability are not opposites, but multipliers. The Gift of Struggle and The Red Helicopter are books that have inspired me, and they are worthwhile companion books on your leadership journey.

In a world full of performance, authenticity is radical. It's not just a leadership style; it's a revolution of presence. When you bring your full self into an organization, you don't just do the job. You change the culture. You light the path. You remind others that power isn't something you chase; it's something you embody.

Notes & Reflections

Notes & Reflections

8

The Real Framework™

Chapter 8: The REAL Framework™

Where your life reflects who you are

To ground myself in intentional self-reflection and an honest internal check-in when needed, I created the REAL framework™. This is my personal operating system for returning to alignment. While many tools focus on productivity or goal setting, REAL centers on energy, identity, and congruence. It's about reclaiming who you already are beneath the roles, expectations, and noise. The framework is a collection of prompts to help me compare my behaviors with my priorities. Every morning, I start my day with journaling, gratitude, prayer, and reflection to set the tone for my day. During seasons when something feels off, when I'm stretched too thin, disconnected, or feeling burnout, I take myself through this framework as an energy audit and reset as part of my daily journal practice. This season of life is career focused for me, so the prompts below are career focused when I complete this exercise. If you are in a career transition, or if you don't work outside the home, respond to the questions in a way that is applicable for your season. REAL stands for the four tenets that define the framework:

- **Reclaim** who you are beneath the roles and expectations
- **Embody** your values consistently and focus on what fuels you
- **Align** your vision, behaviors, and boundaries
- **Lead** with clarity, presence, and action

The REAL Framework™

Where your life reflects who you are

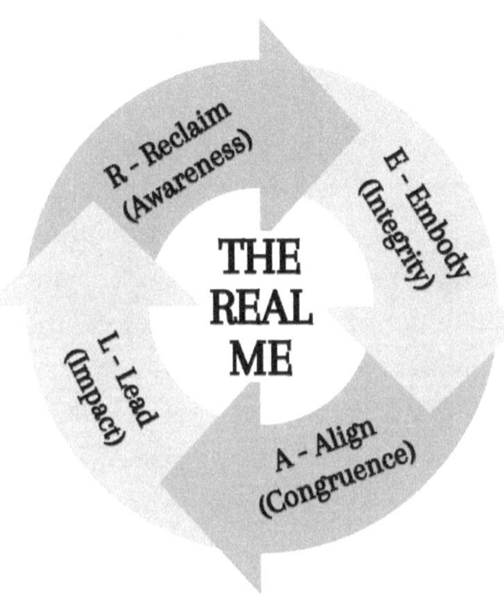

R-Reclaim (Awareness)

Return to who you are beneath roles – find your power

E-Embody (Integrity)

Live your values in daily behavior – what fuels you

A-Align (Congruence)

Adjust choices to match values and energy - connect
the patterns

L-Lead (Impact)

Express your power outward with clarity – action

When authenticity becomes the operating system for leadership, everything changes. And when I talk about leadership, I don't just mean titles or careers, I mean how we lead our lives, our relationships, our energy, and ourselves.

Your Energy

Your energy tells the truth long before your words do. Your energy is one of the most honest indicators of well-being. When you live and lead authentically, your energy flows. You're steady, inspired, and powerful. When you're out of sync, it leaks as resentment, fatigue, overcommitment, burnout, and disconnection.

The REAL Framework™ is an invitation to pause. To observe where your energy goes, what fuels it, and what drains it so you can reclaim your power, embody your truth, align your actions, and lead with purpose. It's a living cycle you can return to anytime you feel stretched, burned out, or in a new season of life.

Step 1: RECLAIM — Find Your Power

It's important to identify where you currently are and what you want to change to plan the way forward. Looking at what drains you can provide key insights about what patterns or roles you may want to change. As you begin this exercise, resist the urge to be judgmental or critical of yourself. The goal is awareness, not perfection.

Reflect:

Think about your week at work, at home, and

within yourself. Where do you feel your energy leaking away? What leaves you mentally, emotionally, or physically exhausted?

Journal Prompts:

- What tasks, roles, or conversations leave me feeling small, tense, or unseen?
- Who or what consistently leaves me drained and emotionally tired?
- What expectations—others' or my own tend to drain me the most?
- Where am I saying "yes" when I really mean "no"?

....

....

....

....

Common Energy Drainers:

- Meetings without meaning
- Constant demand for availability (emails, texts, social pressure)
- People-pleasing and perfectionism
- Lack of creative or restorative time
- Living by "should" instead of "wants"

List your top five energy drainers. These point directly to where boundaries, delegation, conversations, time for rest, or new strategies are needed.

....

....

....

....

....

Step 2: EMBODY — Notice What Fuels You

Now shift your attention to things that bring you joy and inspiration and are in line with your values and priorities. These energy boosters are powerful data points that guide you in the direction you should go.

Reflect:

When do you feel most alive, at peace, creative, or confident? Your body always tells the truth. Notice when your breath deepens, your shoulders relax, and time seems to disappear.

Journal Prompts:

- What moments make me forget to check my phone?
- What am I doing when I feel most like myself?
- Which people, projects, or places leave me feeling refreshed and hopeful?

- What forms of self-expression light me up?

....

....

....

....

....

Common Energy Drivers:
- Deep, meaningful conversations
- Creating something purposeful (music, writing, ideas)
- Mentoring, teaching, or helping others grow
- Time in nature, art, or spiritual practice
- Friendship, laughter, and community

List your **top five energy drivers**. These are indicators of your natural rhythms, values, and zones of purpose.

....

....

....

....

....

Step 3: ALIGN — Connect the Patterns

Alignment is the harmony between who you are and how you move through the world.

Now place your energy drainers and drivers' side by side.
Reflect:
- Where am I spending most of my time and energy?
- How can I create more space for what fuels me?
- Which drainers can I reduce, delegate, redesign, or release?

....

....

....

....

....

Exercise:

- Choose one energy drainer and write a simple plan for how you'll reduce, redesign, or release it this week.
- Choose one thing that brought you joy recently and write how you will intentionally make space for it this week. Alignment doesn't require a complete life overhaul. It begins with conscious adjustments, small decisions that honor what your energy is already telling you.

....

....

....

....

....

Step 4: LEAD with Clarity, Presence, and Aligned Action

Leadership begins with self-trust and the willingness to honor what you already know is true. Let your choices reflect your values.

Reflect:

- List the values that matter most to you right now
- Circle the ones that are non-negotiable

- For each, write what this value looks like in practice in your daily life

....

....

....

....

....

Guiding Questions:
- How can I model the kind of leadership I want to inspire in others?
- Where can I replace reactivity or learned patterns with intention?

....

....

....

....

....

This is where internal alignment becomes visible leadership. When you reclaim your energy, embody your values, align your choices, and lead with intention, you stop outsourcing your power to roles, expectations, or circumstances. You begin to trust your inner signals again. Over time, these small, conscious shifts create a life that feels steadier, more honest, and more fulfilling. Leadership doesn't start with visibility or influence; it starts with authenticity and integrity. And when you lead yourself well, everything else follows

Notes & Reflections

Notes & Reflections

9

Power Through Setbacks

Chapter 9 – Power Through Setbacks

Who you Become as you Rise

"A setback is a setup for a comeback." – JerMarkus

This quote fully resonated with me the first time my friend JerMarkus shared it. I recalled a time I was sitting in the middle of a disappointment I didn't see coming. It was one of those moments where life pulls the rug out from under you, so suddenly that you're still reaching for what used to be there. I remember thinking, 'How could anything good come from this?' But setbacks have a way of teaching you things success never could. They strip away the illusion of control, the performance of strength, and the comfort of certainty. And in the space that remains, you begin to see where your real power lives.

Setbacks aren't always dramatic. Sometimes they come quietly, like a relationship that slowly stops feeling reciprocal, or a job that once energized you but now feels suffocating, and a dream that becomes too heavy to carry the way you've been carrying it. Other times they crash into your life with force. Someone betrays your trust. A promotion goes to someone else. A partnership ends when you thought you were building a future together. These are the moments that shake your identity because they confront the stories you've told yourself about how life should unfold.

Setbacks as Invitations to Pause and Reflect

For years, I assumed setbacks were punishments, signs that I had failed or missed something obvious. However, as I've progressed in my career, I've learned setbacks are often interruptions. They are invitations to pause, reassess, and redirect your energy toward something more fulfilling. They are mirrors that show you what needs healing, what needs strengthening, or what needs to be released. Often, they are detours that protect you from going where you were never meant to settle.

Some of my deepest disappointments came from relationships. There were hurts, inevitable endings, unspoken conversations, and unresolved closures. Nothing destabilizes your sense of power like losing someone you love or trust. But every disappointment taught me something different. They taught me that I can survive endings I didn't ask for, and some lessons are only for much needed redirection.

Navigating Career Setbacks

Career setbacks carry their own sting. I've had several opportunities that slipped away, roles that didn't work out, rooms where I didn't feel seen, and seasons where I questioned whether I still belonged in the spaces I worked so hard to enter. Each time, I felt the weight of disappointment, but I also learned something about authenticity. Sometimes the job you didn't get is the one that would have drained you. Sometimes the door that closed was the one that was leading you away from your purpose. Sometimes the setback simply invites you to re-define success on your own terms.

Resolving career setbacks begins long before the next opportunity appears. It starts with reclaiming your confidence from the situation that shook it. It requires separating your identity from your job title and remembering that your value doesn't disappear because something didn't work out. It means reflecting on what the setback is revealing. Were you somewhere that wasn't a good fit for you? Were you undervalued or underutilized? Were you playing it small to fit in?

From there, you get to rebuild with intention: updating your skills, strengthening your voice, surrounding yourself with mentors who see your potential, and seeking roles that honor your authenticity rather than suppress it. The resolution isn't about rushing to the next thing; it's about rising with more clarity, purpose, and power than you had before.

Defining and Protecting your Identity

One of the most powerful ways to move through setbacks is to anchor your identity beyond a single title or role. I often remind people, and myself to never place your worth in one job, one relationship, or one version of success. Roles can change, seasons can end, and plans can fall apart, but who you are at your core remains. When you develop your life holistically, your purpose becomes portable. I am passionate about supporting the growth of others and witnessing their breakthroughs, and that calling doesn't disappear when a role shifts; it simply finds a new expression. Whether I'm showing up as a wife, a mother, a corporate leader, a nonprofit board member, or a neighbor, my priorities and values flow with me. Setbacks may alter the container, but they don't erase the essence. When you know who you are, you don't lose yourself in transition; you carry yourself forward, stronger and more rooted than before.

Choosing how you Rise

Setbacks challenge your power not because they weaken you, but because they force you to choose how you will rise. And rising requires honesty. It requires allowing yourself to feel the hurt without letting it shape your identity. It requires sitting with the discomfort long enough to understand what it's trying to teach you. It requires choosing respect for yourself even when someone else didn't respect you. It requires choosing purpose even when the path becomes unclear.

The question is not: *How do I avoid setbacks?* The real question is: *Who do I become because of them?*

Presence, Perspective, Peace, and Protection

Power through setbacks begins with presence and acknowledging what happened without denying your feelings. The next step is perspective. Ask yourself: what is this moment revealing? What is it redirecting me toward? What strength is it inviting me to develop? And then comes the most important part: protection. Protecting your peace. Protecting your boundaries. Protecting your self-respect so that the disappointment shapes your wisdom, not your worth.

Holding your power in a setback means refusing to chase what walked away. It means not shrinking yourself to fit someone else's perception of you. It means trusting that the clarity you gain from loss is more valuable than the comfort you gained from the familiar. It means understanding that endings are not failures; they are transitions.

And eventually, sometimes in days, sometimes in months, you begin to see it. The comeback. The new opportunity. The healthier relationship. The direction that feels more you. The version of yourself who is more confident, more grounded, and more certain of what you deserve.

Setbacks don't define you. They refine you. And when you rise authentically, you step into a new level of power. A power rooted in resilience, clarity, and self-respect. This is a power that doesn't depend on circumstances going your way. It's a power that lives in who you become when they don't.

Your comeback doesn't start when everything is fixed. Your comeback starts the moment you decide that even this, *especially this*, will not break your purpose.

A setback is a setup for a comeback. And your next chapter begins the moment you choose to stand back up.

Notes & Reflections

Notes & Reflections

10

Power in the World

Chapter 10 – Power in the World

When Your Life Becomes a Force for Change

There is a moment in your journey when your personal growth stops being only about you. It becomes bigger, wider, deeper, and more expansive. Your alignment, once an internal shift, becomes a public force. Your authenticity becomes influence. Your clarity becomes leadership. Your courage becomes inspiration. And your life and talents lived on purpose, become a ripple effect that reach far beyond your immediate world.

I still remember the excitement of being selected for my school's music program as a first grader. I rushed home from school that day to tell my parents all about it. At that time, I couldn't have imagined how pivotal music would become in my life. I only knew that songs spoke to me deeply, and that I thought in terms of message and melody long before I had the language to explain why.

As a teenager, I began writing songs to process my thoughts and emotions. Music became a place of comfort, healing, and joy. There was something profoundly grounding about completing a song and sharing it with others. Over time, what started as a personal outlet began to expand. My songwriting shifted from self-reflection to curiosity about how music might support others in their own growth and healing.

I came to see music as a universal language, a powerful tool for building meaningful connection and community. My songs evolved from personal, deeply introspective stories to explorations of shared themes and collective journeys. Eventually, that evolution carried my work beyond albums and into online courses and conference workshops. What began as a personal journey became a pathway for impact. The more I leaned into this passion, the clearer it became that its purpose extended far beyond me.

Music has created one pathway for impact and community for me. I invite you to consider your own unique gifts, skills, and talents that create pathways of impact for you. We all have them and it's up to us to discover and nurture them.

Stepping into the Light with Intention

To use your gifts and talents for meaningful impact, you must be willing to step into the light and allow yourself to be seen. That sounds simple, but visibility carries weight. When you show up fully, you invite noise—feedback, opinions, questions, and criticism, alongside encouragement and support.

I'm grateful for my friends who regularly remind me to let myself be fully seen. When they notice me slipping into old habits of staying on the sidelines, they gently call me forward. They're part of my trusted inner circle—the kind of support system that keeps you grounded, protected, and moving forward, even when visibility feels uncomfortable. This is the uplifting kind of friend I mentioned earlier in this book.

Visibility is not about popularity or performance. Visibility is about allowing yourself to be seen so that your gifts can fulfill their purpose. When you step into your authentic voice, you naturally become more visible. You speak up. You take space. You lead. You stop hiding your ideas, your creativity, your calling, or your difference. Visibility requires courage because being seen means being known. If you're not willing to be visible, you limit the impact you're capable of creating. But when you choose to shine, you inspire others to do the same. Your visibility becomes a light post for anyone searching for their own possibility. And with the technology we have today, that light post can shine anywhere in the world, at any time. You can truly impact the world.

Global Impact and Service

The world needs aligned leaders. It needs authentic voices and courageous advocates, people who are grounded and awake enough to influence with wisdom rather than ego.

It needs leaders who move with vision, not fear. People who create change without replicating the harm they've worked so hard to heal. People who dream boldly, think creatively, and pair imagination with the discipline to bring ideas into reality. These are the alchemists of our time. The global changemakers. This is who you become when you honor your power, and this is how your life becomes catalytic.

Who are the people you think of who have inspired you as leaders? What do you admire about them?

There are countless organizations, movements, and people with global impact that started with a single idea or a quiet calling. I draw inspiration from many of them. I'm moved by Brené Brown's teaching on vulnerability and emotional literacy, and by Jay Shetty's mission to make wisdom go viral. I'm inspired by the Nomi Network's commitment to end human trafficking and by Ryan Tedder's songwriting and creative expression. I've learned a great deal from my friend Pat Asp's leadership journey and strategic mindset. I'm still inspired by and owe a great deal to the doctors who helped me through serious respiratory challenges throughout my childhood, and the teachers who guided my path over three decades ago.

So many people offered me courage and perspective because they chose to live with purpose and brought their visions to life. As they lived their purpose, their work reached me. And among all these influences, I also cherish the influence of those closest to home. I'm grateful for my father's thirst for knowledge and understanding, my mother's courage, work ethic, and compassion for others, and my husband's pragmatic approach and steady discipline. Each of them has shaped who I am today in ways I carry with me every day. The impact they have had on me is part of their legacy.

Legacy: The Imprint of a Purposeful Life

We don't often realize or think about this, but our purposeful life is what builds legacy. Legacy is not what you leave behind when you die; it is what you build every day through the way you live, love, and lead.

Your legacy is shaped not by grand gestures, but by consistent action. When you choose purpose over fear, truth over approval, boundaries over burnout, and impact over image, you are building a legacy of greatness. You become a person whose life changes other people's lives. Legacy is:

- the lives you touched
- the opportunities you created
- the ideas you sparked
- the resilience you modeled
- the healing you initiated
- the courage you embodied
- the systems you improved
- the communities you strengthened
- the impact you made by living authentically

Power in the world is not something you chase—it is something you embody. And when you embody it, your life becomes a movement. You expand beyond your own story and become part of something larger: a lineage of people who created change simply by being brave enough to live their truth.

Notes & Reflections

11

Power, on Purpose

Chapter 11: Power, on Purpose

A Life of Fulfillment and Impact

As you arrive at this final chapter, my hope is that something in these pages has stayed with you. Maybe a tool felt especially helpful, or a story stirred something you hadn't fully named before. Maybe a section felt uncomfortable or out of place. That's worth paying attention to, too. Often, what unsettles us is just asking to be explored more gently and more honestly.

I also hope that whatever prompted you to pick up this book—curiosity, exhaustion, longing, or a quiet inner nudge, has been met here in some meaningful way. Think of this book not as an ending, but as a stepping-stone. A place to pause, reflect, and then continue forward with more awareness than you had before.

This is the beginning of living your *Power, on Purpose*.

Everything you've read so far has been guiding you back to yourself. Back to who you are beneath conditioning, expectations, people-pleasing, and survival patterns. Along the way, you've explored how to strengthen your voice, honor your boundaries, protect your energy, choose healthy relationships, and show up with greater presence and clarity. We've explored authenticity not as a trend or personality trait, but as a daily commitment.

Now, standing at the threshold of what comes next, you get to decide how you want to live from here. Because *Power, on Purpose* isn't just an idea. It's a way of moving through the world with intention rather than reaction, clarity rather than confusion, and fulfillment rather than self-abandonment.

A Life you Design, not one you Inherit

Every day, whether we realize it or not, we're either living by design or by default. We're either making conscious choices, or replaying patterns that we inherited, absorbed, or learned to survive. Most of us begin life on autopilot by fulfilling roles, meeting expectations, and staying in the systems that reward compliance more than authenticity.

Things begin to shift when we pause long enough to ask honest questions. *Is this belief really mine? Is this obligation aligned with who I'm becoming? Is this path still true for me?*

A *Power, on Purpose* life doesn't require that you have everything figured out. It simply means your choices are intentional and no longer accidental. You stop performing and start designing. You begin choosing what nourishes you, what supports your peace, what honors your values and goals, and what strengthens your sense of purpose.

Using Your Voice with Intention

Your voice is one of your most powerful tools to build understanding, bring clarity, and speak truth where it's needed. When your voice comes from your power rather than fear, it becomes steady and trustworthy. It carries confidence without force and compassion without compromise. And something important happens on the way. Each time you speak honestly, you reinforce your self-respect. Each time you advocate for yourself, you strengthen your identity. Each time you communicate with intention, your relationships deepen.

Your voice doesn't just shape the world around you. It reshapes the relationship you have with yourself. Used well, it becomes part of your legacy.

Boundaries, Peace, and the Stewardship of Your Energy

One of the most meaningful shifts in a *Power, on Purpose* life is learning to treat your energy as something sacred—because it is. Your energy holds your creativity, intuition, clarity, and capacity to give and receive love. When it's constantly drained, distracted, or dictated by external expectations, you lose access to the parts of yourself that matter most.

Boundaries, as we've discussed, aren't walls. They're a quiet, consistent practice of choosing yourself without guilt. They bring clarity about what sustains you, what depletes you, what you can hold, and what you're no longer meant to carry. As you honor your boundaries, you protect the person you're becoming and protect your energy. And as you protect your peace, your presence naturally grows more grounded and powerful.

This is how life shifts from something you endure to something you lead.

Clarity and the Opportunities Meant for You

One of the most liberating truths of alignment is this: people who are centered don't chase everything and everyone. When you know who you are, it becomes easier to recognize what belongs to you and what doesn't need to. Opportunities stop feeling overwhelming because you can sense the difference between what's right for you and what's simply available.

As your clarity deepens, so does your presence. Your values become visible. Your boundaries become understood. People know how to approach you, what you stand for, and where your yes truly lives. Just as importantly, your no becomes clear and grounded. Clarity creates coherence and fuels momentum. It anchors your reputation and makes your path feel steady, even when it's evolving.

As you live with greater clarity and intention, your chosen community begins to reflect your values and priorities. You make space for genuine, meaningful relationships where mutual learning can take root—where we reflect truth to one another, challenge each other with care, and inspire growth by being real. Kim Cummings is a dear friend and a woman I deeply admire. As part of a trusted focus group who walked alongside me while I explored the themes of this book, Kim shared a beautiful perspective that deeply touched me.

"I spent years believing that being first at everything was the silent crown I earned, only to discover I had quietly placed myself last. Your words struck me in that uncomfortable space where truth lives—the realization that 'making time for what matters' was never about fitting everything in, but about finally including myself in that equation. As a mom and executive, I see now that the invisible crown we wear isn't a badge of honor; it's a weight we're allowed to set down. Your journey gave me permission to reimagine what it means to pour into others by first pouring into myself. And here's what I'm learning about leadership: people don't remember every decision I made or every process I perfected—they remember whether I showed up as my authentic self. The most powerful thing we can do as leaders isn't to have all the answers or do everything flawlessly; it's to be real enough that others feel permission to do the same. That uncomfortable truth? That is where transformation begins." *Kim Cummings*

I felt every word she shared and recognized myself in her experience. Sharing our experiences and lessons strengthened both of us.

A Commitment to Yourself

As you close this book, I invite you to make a meaningful commitment to yourself. A commitment to live with greater awareness, to protect your peace, and to honor your boundaries. A commitment to speak with clarity and compassion and to choose opportunities that align with who you are becoming. A commitment to love yourself boldly and without apology.

Most of all, a commitment to no longer dim your light to fit into spaces you've outgrown.

Your life is waiting. Your purpose has been calling. And from this moment forward, may you walk into every room, every relationship, every opportunity—not as someone performing for approval, but as someone living fully in their *Power, on Purpose*

Notes & Reflections

Notes & Reflections

Notes & Reflections

Notes & Reflections

Notes & Reflections

Notes & Reflections

Notes & Reflections

Notes & Reflections

Notes & Reflections

Notes & Reflections

Notes & Reflections

Notes & Reflections

Notes & Reflections

Notes & Reflections

Notes & Reflections

Notes & Reflections

Notes & Reflections

Notes & Reflections

Notes & Reflections

Notes & Reflections

Notes & Reflections

Notes & Reflections

Notes & Reflections

Notes & Reflections

Notes & Reflections

Alignment

The lived experience of your values and decisions agreeing with each other so that your priorities, choices and actions reflect who you really are.

Alignment Over Adaptation

Choosing authenticity and integrity over reshaping yourself to meet external expectations, approval, or survival-based patterns.

Authenticity

Consistency between your inner truth and your outer expression, even when it feels uncomfortable or countercultural.

Boundaries

Clear, compassionate limits that protect your energy, values, and well-being while honoring both self-respect and mutual respect.

Congruence

When your energy, words, and boundaries send the same message.

Emotional Power/Regulation

The ability to feel deeply without reacting impulsively.

Freedom
The internal and external capacity to choose your responses, direction, and priorities without being driven by fear, guilt, or expectation.

Healthy Endings
The ability to conclude relationships, roles, or chapters with clarity, dignity, and integrity, even when closure is imperfect or one-sided.

Identity (Beyond Roles)
An understanding of who you are apart from titles, achievements, relationships, or seasons of life, allowing your core self to flow across all roles.

Integrity
Consistency between values, words, and actions, especially when the cost feels high.

People-pleasing
Negotiating your truth in exchange for approval.

Power
The conscious, grounded ability to choose, influence, and act in alignment with your values.

Power, on Purpose
The intentional use of your voice, influence, and energy in ways that are values-driven, aligned, and rooted in self-awareness rather than fear or performance.

Purpose
An evolving expression of your gifts, values, and contribution, revealed through lived experience rather than a single destination or role.

Radical Leadership
Leading from your inner truth in systems built for performance.

Self-Mastery
The practice of regulating your thoughts, emotions, and behaviors so you can respond with intention rather than habit or conditioning.

Unlearning
The conscious process of releasing inherited beliefs, roles, and coping mechanisms that once protected you but no longer serve who you are becoming.

Wholeness
Allowing all parts of yourself—strength, vulnerability, creativity, ambition, and rest to coexist without fragmentation or shame.

Referenced and Recommended Material

Brown, B. (2021). *Atlas of the Heart: Mapping Meaningful Connection and the Language of Human Experience*. Random House. Page 28

Chamine, S. (2012). *Positive Intelligence: Why Only 20% of Teams and Individuals Achieve Their True Potential—and How You Can Achieve Yours*. Greenleaf Book Group Press. Page 24

Clason, G. S. (1926). *The Richest Man in Babylon*. George S. Clason. Page 58

Cloud, H., & Townsend, J. (1992). *Boundaries: When to Say Yes, How to Say No to Take Control of Your Life*. Zondervan. Pages 36–37

Foroux, D. (2024). *The Stoic Path to Wealth: Ancient Wisdom for Enduring Prosperity*. Portfolio / Penguin. Page 59

García, H., & Miralles, F. (2017). *Ikigai: The Japanese Secret to a Long and Happy Life*. Penguin Books. Page 18

Goleman, D. (1995). *Emotional Intelligence: Why It Can Matter More Than IQ*. Bantam Books. Page 38

Herrera, B. (2023). *The Gift of Struggle: Life-Changing Lessons About Leading*. Bard Press. Page 70

Rhee, J. (2021). *Red Helicopter: Lead Change with Kindness (Plus a Little Math)*. Wiley. Page 70

Robbins, M. (2023). *The Let Them Theory*. Hay House. Page 47

Robin, V., & Domínguez, J. (2018). *Your Money or Your Life: 9 Steps to Transforming Your Relationship with Money and Achieving Financial Independence* (Revised and updated ed.). Penguin Books. (Original work published 1992) Page 58

Acknowledgements

This book did not come to life in isolation.

To the focus group participants who read early drafts and offered thoughtful, honest feedback—thank you. Your insights and lived experiences helped shape these pages and kept this work grounded.

To my children, my most honest editors—thank you for your curiosity, your questions, and your ability to let me know when something didn't sound like *me*. To my husband for your constant support. Your perspectives brought both clarity and heart to this process.

I'm grateful to the mentors, leaders, and authors whose work has influenced my thinking and deepened my understanding of leadership and personal growth. Your ideas were steady companions throughout the writing of this book.

To my friends and community—thank you for the support, encouragement, conversations, and belief that carried me through.

And to you, the reader—thank you for choosing this book. If these pages support you in reclaiming your power, navigating growth with intention, and leading your life on purpose, then this work has fulfilled its purpose.

About the Author: Kimia Penton is a leadership speaker, musician, and organizational psychology professional who believes power is meant to be lived, not performed. With experience leading global teams in a Fortune 10 organization, teaching at the university level, and sharing stories on stages as both a keynote speaker and recording artist, she weaves strategy and creativity into work that invites real transformation. Through her REAL framework™—Reclaim, Embody, Align, Lead, her online courses on Authenticity, her original music and workshops, Kimia helps leaders, creatives, and high-achievers build purposeful and fulfilling careers while leading with clarity, courage, heart, and fun!

Learn more at: www.kimiapenton.com

www.linkedin.com/in/kimiapenton/

Instagram: @kimiapenton   Spotify: Kimia Penton

Contact: contact@kimiapenton.com

www.ingramcontent.com/pod-product-compliance
Lightning Source LLC
Chambersburg PA
CBHW062213150726
47991CB00006B/2256